FAST CARS, FAST DRIVERS

KEITH WEST

Contents

The first cars were built over one hundred years ago. The dream was to drive as fast as 60 miles per hour.

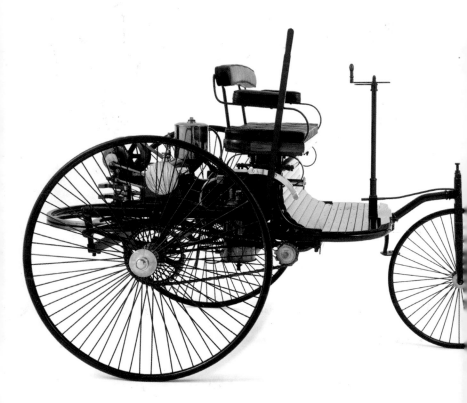

This was one of the first cars ever made, in 1886.

Sixty years ago, this Jaguar sports car could reach a speed of 120 miles per hour.

We've come a long way since then.
Today, designers are working on cars that will go faster than 280 miles per hour.

Would *you* like to drive a car that could go so fast?

For those who enjoy the thrill of speed, this book is for you!

Mercedes 35 HP

This car was made in Germany in 1901. It was the first car built for speed, rather than just for people to travel in.

In fact, it was the first sports car.

BMW 328

The BMW 328 was built in 1936. This car was much lighter and faster than its rivals.

Its top speed was 94 miles per hour.

Did you know?

In 1976, BMW made the car again.
It looked a lot like the first model but had the power and speed of a much later car.

Cisitalia 202 Grand Sport

This beautiful car was made in Italy.

The light, clever design helped it reach almost 100 miles per hour.

People loved the design of this car. One model was even displayed at the Museum of Modern Art in New York!

Mercedes-Benz 300 SL

This was the dream car of the 1950s. Most people called it the "Gullwing". The doors opened upwards, so they looked a bit like the wings of a seagull.

Its top speed was 140 miles per hour. That even makes it a fast car today – but for the 1950s it was amazing. Now it would cost you nearly one million pounds to buy.

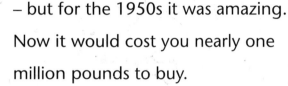

Today, the fastest and most expensive cars are called "supercars". Here are two of the most famous ones.

Lamborghini Reventon

Lamborghini made this car to look like a **supersonic** fighter jet. (Supersonic means faster than the speed of sound.) The Reventon is the most expensive car Lamborghini has ever made. All of the cars are silver on the outside with black wheels.

Get the stats

Made in: 2007

Acceleration: 0 to 60 miles per hour in just over 3 seconds

Top speed: 221 miles per hour

This is the second most expensive car you can buy today. Only twenty were ever made.

It once raced a Tornado fighter plane on a runway.

The car led for most of the race, but the fighter plane won ... by just a few metres!

Aston Martin One-77

This is the fastest car ever made by the British firm Aston Martin – and the most expensive.

From the start, Aston Martin said they would only ever make seventy-seven of them. That's why it's called the One-77. Only the very rich can afford one!

Get the stats

Price: £1.2 million

acceleration: 0 to 60 miles per hour in 3.5 seconds

Top speed: 220 miles per hour

With the One-77, Aston Martin set out to build a car that used all the latest technology. Experts built it by hand.

It's fast.

It's powerful.

It's beautiful.

You could say that the Aston Martin One-77 is the "King of the Supercar".

"Grand Prix" means "Grand Prize" in French.

The very first Grand Prix motor race took place in France, in 1906. Thirty-two cars raced for twelve laps of nearly 65 miles each. The race took two days to complete and the average speed of the fastest car was just over 62 miles per hour.

As you can see, the cars looked very different in those days.

What is Formula One?

Today, the top motor-racing cars are called Formula One, or F1 for short. Formula One racing began in 1950. The Grand Prix races take place in different countries all over the world.

Drivers need to gain experience by winning races in other competitions before they are allowed to race in Formula One.

Formula One: The Races

Here you can see all the Grand Prix races that take place in a year. It's a busy life!

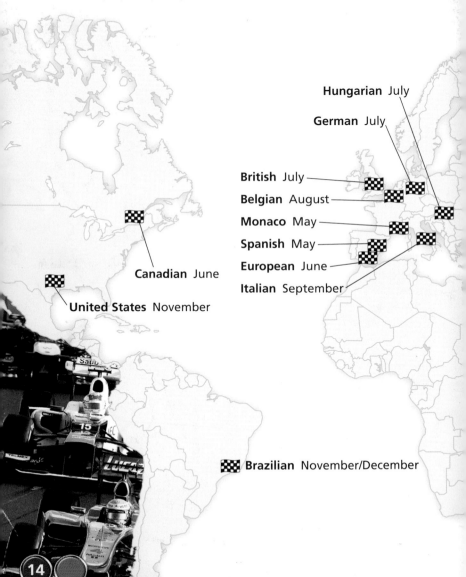

Hungarian July

German July

British July

Belgian August

Monaco May

Spanish May

European June

Italian September

Canadian June

United States November

Brazilian November/December

Chinese April

Bahrain April

Abu Dhabi November

 **Japanese** October

Korean October

Indian October

Malaysian March

Singapore September

Australian March

Making a Formula One car

A Formula One car is built for one thing – speed!

It will only win races if it is very carefully designed. It has to be the best.

Designers use the most up-to-date computer software to design each part of the car.

The **chassis** is made from a single piece of material. It must be very light, for maximum speed.

chassis the frame of a motor car

A Formula One engine runs at a very high speed. This produces a lot of heat, and heat ruins the engine.

As a result, a Formula One engine only lasts for about 500 miles. Most Grand Prix races are about 190 miles long, plus the practice laps. So the engine needs to be changed for just about every race.

Formula One: Behind the scenes

Formula One teams design and build the cars. They also employ the drivers. For example, Lewis Hamilton drives for McLaren.

Every season is different. Slight changes to the Formula One rules mean that designers have to develop new cars every year.

Crash tests

Before the first race of the year, the new cars for the season have to be crash-tested. This is to show they are safe to drive.

Crash tests take place on the front, back and sides of every new Formula One car. The driver's area needs to stay completely safe for the car to pass the test.

Here is a Formula One car being crash-tested in the factory.

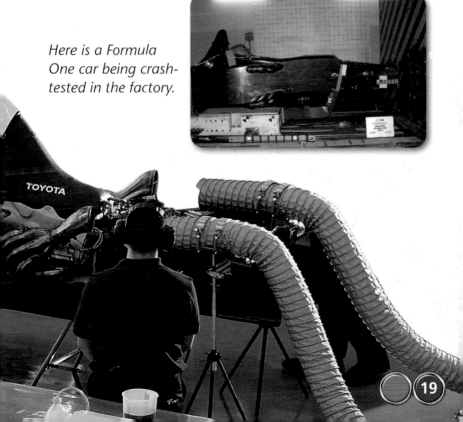

Formula One stats

In the World Championship series, drivers gain points for each race. The driver with the most points at the end of the season becomes World Champion.

A German driver, Michael Schumacher, has won the World Championship seven times. Nobody has yet matched his record!

Which country has produced the most drivers?

The UK has produced the most drivers: 150 since the first Grand Prix in 1950. Here are some of the most famous British drivers.

Stirling Moss   Damon Hill   Jackie Stewart

Who is the youngest ever Grand Prix winner?

Sebastian Vettel of Germany was the youngest ever winner. He was just twenty-one when he won his first Grand Prix.

Having a winning team

Winning is not just about the drivers. It's also about the people behind the scenes.

Formula One pit crews have to train like top sportsmen. Each car will need its tyres changed two or three times in a race, as quickly as possible. Every second counts.

An 18-man crew can change all four tyres in just 1.8 seconds!

Formula One: The teams

There are three British racing teams:

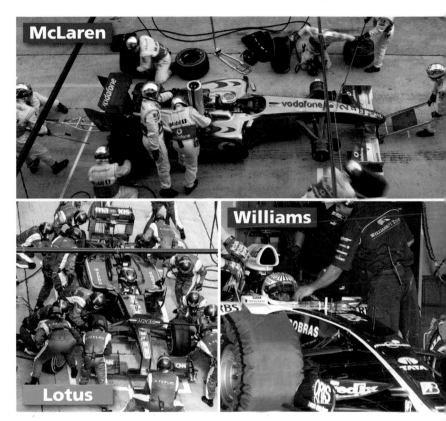

Each of their cars has the team's colours.

Another successful team is Red Bull. In 2011, they were almost unbeatable. They are an Austrian team, but they are based in Britain.

Jenson Button

Jenson began karting when he was just eight years old.

Junior karting

He won the British Super Prize and went on to win all 34 races of the 1991 Cadet Kart Championship.

Jenson moved on to Formula One in 2000. He won the Grand Prix World Championship in 2009, driving for Honda. In 2010, he moved to McLaren.

Lewis Hamilton

Lewis was seen as a future winner as early as 2004, when he was just 19. The Williams team wanted to sign him as their driver, but their engine supplier refused to support him.

In fact, Lewis wanted to drive for McLaren. He started Formula One driving in 2007. In his first season, he came second, and he won the World Championship the next year.

In 2012, he is still driving for McLaren.

Sebastian Vettel

Sebastian drives for Red Bull and has won two World Championships in a row.

In 2011, Sebastian won 11 races and he won the World Championship with several races still to go.

Ayrton Senna

Motor racing is a very dangerous sport, even with all the safety checks. In 1994, the Brazilian driver Ayrton Senna had a huge crash and died in a Grand Prix race. Since then, safety checks have been even more strict.

Ayrton Senna had been World Champion three times.

The Dakar Rally

The Dakar Rally is extreme. Only the very brave and tough can win!

The rally is held every year. It's an off-road race and anyone can take part in it, if you have a suitable vehicle. Drivers sometimes cover up to 500 miles a day, crossing mud, desert or rocks.

The race used to run from France to Senegal, in West Africa.

Since 1998, the rally has been held in South America. Motorbikes, cars and trucks take part and the race lasts 15 days!

Like Formula One races, it can be very dangerous. In 2012, one biker was killed and a French biker was badly injured.

The Indianapolis 500

The biggest motor race in the USA is the Indianapolis 500, usually called the "Indy 500". It is held during the last weekend of May.

The drivers race for 500 miles, which is 200 times round the track.

It is considered even more dangerous than Formula One.

There are more cars in the race.

The track is a lot shorter.

The Land Speed Record

Andy Green is a fighter pilot for the British Royal Air Force. He's also interested in setting records.

On 15 September 1997, Andy was the first person to drive a car faster than the speed of sound.

His car was the ThrustSSC. That stands for Thrust **SuperSonic** Car.

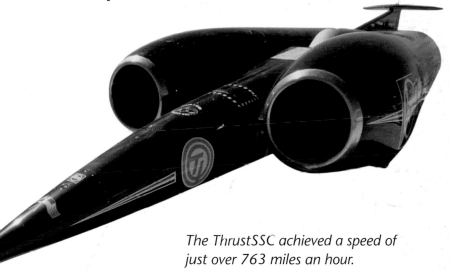

The ThrustSSC achieved a speed of just over 763 miles an hour.

supersonic faster than the speed of sound

Stunt driving

Stunt drivers do crazy and dangerous things.

Driving off huge ramps at high speeds

Driving through fire

Jumping over lines of parked cars

In this scene from the film Transporter 3, *actor Jason Statham does his own driving stunt.*

Skiing is when a car is driven on just two wheels.

How is it done?

The stunt is usually done by driving one pair of wheels up a ramp, which then lifts the side of the car.

Some stunt drivers make money by driving dangerously in films.

Ben is a racing driver *and* a
stunt driver.

You may have seen him drive
as "The Stig" in the programme
Top Gear. For a long time,
no one knew who The Stig
really was.

In fact, Ben has competed in
motor racing for nearly 20 years.

Ben was the driving double for actor Daniel Craig in the James Bond films *Quantum of Solace* and *Casino Royale*. He did the same for Christian Bale in the Batman film *The Dark Knight Rises*.

Turn over to read the interview.

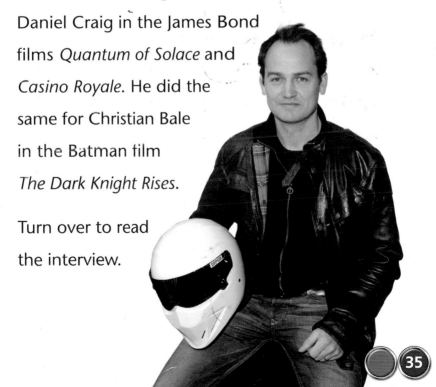

What's the fastest car you've driven?

A Bugatti Veyron Super Sport – at 267 miles an hour!

Any "cool" crashes?

Every one I walked away from! One crash on *Top Gear* was funny, but only after it happened. At the time, I felt terrible for damaging an expensive car; it was worth not far off a million dollars. I thought I was going to get fired!

Who's your favourite racing driver and why?

Ayrton Senna was my hero because whenever he drove, it was something special. He always seemed to be pushing himself and the car a little harder than everyone else.

Have you ever driven a motorbike? If so, what did it feel like?

I rode a bike, fell off, and it hurt. Tried it again recently – went really fast, fell off, and it hurt again.

Finally, what advice would you give to any young person who wanted to get into motorsport?

Never give up. It's true in real life, and just as true with every race you ever enter. Never stop challenging yourself and your competitors because you make your own luck.

Reader challenge

Word hunt

1 On page 12, find a verb that means "finish".

2 On page 22, find a noun made of two words.

Text sense

3 When did Jenson Button start Formula One driving? (page 24)

4 What happened to Ayrton Senna in 1994? (page 27)

5 Why is the Dakar Rally called an "extreme" race? (page 28)

6 Why do you think stunt drivers are willing to do dangerous things? (pages 32–33)

7 Why do you think *Top Gear* didn't tell anyone who The Stig was? (page 34)

Your views

9 What skills would you need to be a Formula One driver? Give reasons.

10 Did you enjoy reading this book? Give reasons.

Spell it

With a partner, look at these words and then cover them up.

- fastest
- lightest
- toughest

Take it in turns for one of you to read the words aloud. The other person has to try and spell each word. Check your answers, then swap over.

Try it

With a partner, imagine you are film directors. Design a stunt to include in an action film where two cars are racing each other.

William Collins's dream of knowledge for all began with the publication of his first book in 1819. A self-educated mill worker, he not only enriched millions of lives, but also founded a flourishing publishing house. Today, staying true to this spirit, Collins books are packed with inspiration, innovation and practical expertise. They place you at the centre of a world of possibility and give you exactly what you need to explore it.

Collins. Freedom to teach.

Published by Collins Education
An imprint of HarperCollins*Publishers*
77–85 Fulham Palace Road, Hammersmith, London W6 8JB

Browse the complete Collins Education catalogue at **www.collinseducation.com**

Text by Keith West © HarperCollins Publishers Limited 2012

Series consultants: Alan Gibbons and Natalie Packer

10 9 8 7 6 5 4 3 2 1
ISBN 978-0-00-748892-6

British Library Cataloguing in Publication Data.
A catalogue record for this publication is available from the British Library.

Commissioned by Catherine Martin

Edited and project-managed by Sue Chapple

Picture research and proofreading by Grace Glendinning

Design and typesetting by Jordan Publishing Design Limited

Cover design by Paul Manning

Acknowledgements

The publishers would like to express their thanks to Ben Collins for the interview on pages 36–37.

The publishers would like to thank the students and teachers of the following schools for their help in trialling the Read On series:

Southfields Academy, London
Queensbury School, Queensbury, Bradford
Langham C of E Primary School, Langham, Rutland
Ratton School, Eastbourne, East Sussex
Northfleet School for Girls, North Fleet, Kent
Westergate Community School, Chichester, West Sussex
Bottesford C of E Primary School, Bottesford, Nottinghamshire
Woodfield Academy, Redditch, Worcestershire
St Richard's Catholic College, Bexhill, East Sussex

The publishers gratefully acknowledge the permission granted to reproduce the copyright material in this book. While every effort has been made to trace and contact copyright holders, where this has not been possible the publishers will be pleased to make the necessary arrangements at the first opportunity.

The publisher would like to thank the following for permission to reproduce pictures in these pages (t = top, b = bottom, c = centre, l = left, r = right):

p 2 Simon Clay/Getty Images, p 3 EML/Shutterstock, p 4 The Print Collector/Alamy, p 5 KENCKOphotography/Shutterstock, p 7t Tom Wood/Alamy, p 7b Rob Marson/Flickr, pp 8–9 Taco Ekkel/WikiMedia Commons, p 9 Lamborghini, pp 10–11 cmonville/Flickr, p 12 WikiMedia Commons, p 13 PAUL CROCK/AFP/Getty Images, p 14 WILLIAM WEST/AFP/Getty Images, p 15 Peter J Fox/Getty Images, p 16 Sutton/Sutton Images/Corbis, p 17 Steve Nickolas/Alamy, pp 18–19 Stuart Franklin/Getty Images, p 19 Sutton/Sutton Images/Corbis, p 20 Clive Mason/ALLSPORT/Getty Images, p 21cl Klemantaski Collection/Getty Images, p 21cr Rolls Press/Popperfoto/Getty Images, p 21cc Mike Hewitt/Allsport/Getty Images, p 21b JUNG YEON-JE/AFP/Getty Images, p 22 CHEN WS/Shutterstock, p 23cr David Acosta Allely/Shutterstock, p 23cl cjmac/Shutterstock, p 23t CHEN WS/Shutterstock, p 24c Jaggat/Shutterstock, p 24t DSPA/Shutterstock, p 25 Paul Gilham/Getty Images, p 26 Mark Thompson/Getty Images, p 27 Anton Want/ALLSPORT/Getty Images, p 28 SÃjgi ElemÃ©r/Shutterstock, pp 28–29 Christian Vinces/Shutterstock, p 30 Sutton/Sutton Images/Corbis, p 31 David Madison/Getty Images, p 32t Ryhor M Zasinets/Shutterstock, p 32c PhotoStock10/Shutterstock, p 32b Herbie Knott/Rex Features, p 33 c.Lions Gate/Everett/Rex Features, p 34 AlamyCelebrity/Alamy, p 35t Kris Connor/Getty Images, p 35b AlamyCelebrity/Alamy, p 36 Max Earey/Shutterstock.